Electric
Light

●

●

●

SEAMUS HEANEY

Electric

Light

Farrar, Straus and Giroux

New York

•

•

•

FARRAR, STRAUS AND GIROUX

19 Union Square West, New York 10003

Originally published in 2001 by Faber and Faber Ltd., Great Britain

Published in the United States by Farrar, Straus and Giroux

First American edition, 2001

Library of Congress Cataloging-in-Publication Data

Heaney, Seamus.

　　Electric light / Seamus Heaney.— 1st American ed.

　　p.　cm.

　　ISBN 0-374-14683-7 (alk. paper)

　　I. Title.

　　PR6058.E2 E37 2001

　　821'.914—dc21

　　　　　　　　　　　　00-067278

Designed by Margaret M. Wagner

For Matthew and Caroline

CONTENTS

•

•

•

I

II

At Toomebridge

Where the flat water
Came pouring over the weir out of Lough Neagh
As if it had reached an edge of the flat earth
And fallen shining to the continuous
Present of the Bann.
                              Where the checkpoint used to be.
Where the rebel boy was hanged in '98.
Where negative ions in the open air
Are poetry to me. As once before
The slime and silver of the fattened eel.

Perch

Perch on their water-perch hung in the clear Bann River
Near the clay bank in alder-dapple and waver,

Perch we called "grunts," little flood-slubs, runty and ready,
I saw and I see in the river's glorified body

That is passable through, but they're bluntly holding the pass,
Under the water-roof, over the bottom, adoze,

Guzzling the current, against it, all muscle and slur
In the finland of perch, the fenland of alder, on air

That is water, on carpets of Bann stream, on hold
In the everything flows and steady go of the world.

Lupins

They stood. And stood for something. Just by standing.
In waiting. Unavailable. But there
For sure. Sure and unbending.
Rose-fingered dawn's and navy midnight's flower.

Seed packets to begin with, pink and azure,
Sifting lightness and small jittery promise:
Lupin spires, erotics of the future,
Lip-brush of the blue and earth's deep purchase.

O pastel turrets, pods and tapering stalks
That stood their ground for all our summer wending
And even when they blanched would never balk.
And none of this surpassed our understanding.

Out of the Bag

All of us came in Doctor Kerlin's bag.
He'd arrive with it, disappear to the room
And by the time he'd reappear to wash

Those nosy, rosy, big, soft hands of his
In the scullery basin, its lined insides
(The colour of a spaniel's inside lug)

Were empty for all to see, the trap-sprung mouth
Unsnibbed and gaping wide. Then like a hypnotist
Unwinding us, he'd wind the instruments

Back into their lining, tie the cloth
Like an apron round itself,
Darken the door and leave

With the bag in his hand, a plump ark by the keel . . .
Until the next time came and in he'd come
In his fur-lined collar that was also spaniel-coloured

And go stooping up to the room again, a whiff
Of disinfectant, a Dutch interior gleam
Of waistcoat satin and highlights on the forceps.

Getting the water ready, that was next—
Not plumping hot, and not lukewarm, but soft,
Sud-luscious, saved for him from the rain-butt

And savoured by him afterwards, all thanks
Denied as he towelled hard and fast,
Then held his arms out suddenly behind him

To be squired and silk-lined into the camel coat.
At which point he once turned his eyes upon me,
Hyperborean, beyond-the-north-wind blue,

Two peepholes to the locked room I saw into
Every time his name was mentioned, skimmed
Milk and ice, swabbed porcelain, the white

And chill of tiles, steel hooks, chrome surgery tools
And blood dreeps in the sawdust where it thickened
At the foot of each cold wall. And overhead

The little, pendent, teat-hued infant parts
Strung neatly from a line up near the ceiling—
A toe, a foot and shin, an arm, a cock

A bit like the rosebud in his buttonhole.

■

Poeta doctus Peter Levi says
Sanctuaries of Asclepius (called *asclepions*)
Were the equivalent of hospitals

In ancient Greece. Or of shrines like Lourdes,
Says *poeta doctus* Graves. Or of the cure
By poetry that cannot be coerced,

Say I, who realized at Epidaurus
That the whole place was a sanatorium
With theatre and gymnasium and baths,

A site of incubation, where "incubation"
Was technical and ritual, meaning sleep
When epiphany occurred and you met the god . . .

Hatless, groggy, shadowing myself
As the thurifer I was in an open air procession
In Lourdes in '56

When I nearly fainted from the heat and fumes,
Again I nearly fainted as I bent
To pull a bunch of grass and hallucinated

Doctor Kerlin at the steamed-up glass
Of our scullery window, starting in to draw
With his large pink index finger dot-faced men

With button-spots in a straight line down their fronts
And women with dot breasts, giving them all
A set of droopy sausage-arms and legs

That soon began to run. And then as he dipped and laved
In the generous suds again, *miraculum*:
The baby bits all came together swimming

Into his soapy big hygienic hands
And I myself came to, blinded with sweat,
Blinking and shaky in the windless light.

III

Bits of the grass I pulled I posted off
To one going into chemotherapy
And one who had come through. I didn't want

To leave the place or link up with the others.
It was mid-day, mid-May, pre-tourist sunlight
In the precincts of the god,

The very site of the temple of Asclepius.
I wanted nothing more than to lie down
Under hogweed, under seeded grass

And to be visited in the very eye of the day
By Hygeia, his daughter, her name still clarifying
The haven of light she was, the undarkening door.

IV

The room I came from and the rest of us all came from
Stays pure reality where I stand alone,
Standing the passage of time, and she's asleep

In sheets put on for the doctor, wedding presents
That showed up again and again, bridal
And usual and useful at births and deaths.

Me at the bedside, incubating for real,
Peering, appearing to her as she closes
And opens her eyes, then lapses back

Into a faraway smile whose precinct of vision
I would enter every time, to assist and be asked
In that hoarsened whisper of triumph,

"And what do you think
Of the new wee baby the doctor brought for us all
When I was asleep?"

Bann Valley Eclogue

Sicelides Musae, paulo maiora canamus
                —VIRGIL, Eclogue IV

POET: Bann Valley Muses, give us a song worth singing,
              Something that rises like the curtain in
              Those words *And it came to pass* or *In the beginning.*
              Help me to please my hedge-schoolmaster Virgil
              And the child that's due. Maybe, heavens, sing
              Better times for her and her generation.

VIRGIL: Here are my words you'll have to find a place for:
              Carmen, ordo, nascitur, saeculum, gens.
              Their gist in your tongue and province should be clear
              Even at this stage. Poetry, order, the times,
              The nation, wrong and renewal, then an infant birth
              And a flooding away of all the old miasma.

              Whatever stains you, you rubbed it into yourselves:
              Earth mark, birth mark, mould like the bloodied mould
              On Romulus's ditch-back. But when the waters break
              Bann's stream will overflow, the old markings
              Will avail no more to keep east bank from west.
              The valley will be washed like the new baby.

POET: *Pacatum orbem*: your words are too much nearly.
              Even "orb" by itself. What on earth could match it?
              And then, last month, at noon-eclipse, wind dropped.

A millennial chill, birdless and dark, prepared.
A firstness steadied, a lastness, a born awareness
As name dawned into knowledge: I saw the orb.

VIRGIL: Eclipses won't be for this child. The cool she'll know
Will be the pram hood over her vestal head.
Big dog daisies will get fanked up in the spokes.
She'll lie on summer evenings listening to
A chug and slug going on in the milking parlour.
Let her never hear close gunfire or explosions.

POET: Why do I remember St. Patrick's mornings,
Being sent by my mother to the railway line
For the little trefoil, untouchable almost, the shamrock
With its twining, binding, creepery, tough, thin roots
All over the place, in the stones between the sleepers.
Dew-scales shook off the leaves. Tear-ducts asperging.

Child on the way, it won't be long until
You land among us. Your mother's showing signs,
Out for her sunset walk among big round bales.
Planet earth like a teething ring suspended
Hangs by its world-chain. Your pram waits in the corner.
Cows are let out. They're sluicing the milk-house floor.

Montana

The stable door was open, the upper half,
When I looked back. I was five years old
And Dologhan stood watching me go off,
John Dologhan, the best milker ever

To come about the place. He sang
"The Rose of Mooncoin" with his head to the cow's side.
He would spin his table knife and when the blade
Stopped with its point towards me, a bright path

Opened between us like a recognition
That made no sense, like my memory of him standing
Behind the half door, holding up the winkers.
Even then he was like an apparition,

A rambler from the Free State and a gambler,
All eyes as the pennies rose and slowed
On Sunday mornings under Butler's Bridge
And downed themselves into that tight-bunched crowd

Of the pitch-and-toss school. Sunlight on far lines,
On the creosoted sleepers and hot stones.
And Dologhan, who'd worked in Montana once,
With the whole day off, in the cool shade of the arch.

The Loose Box

Back at the dark end, slats angled tautly down
From a breast-high beam to the foot of the stable wall—
Silked and seasoned timber of the hayrack.

Marsupial brackets . . . And a deep-littered silence
Off odourless, untainting, fibrous horsedung.

·

On an old recording Patrick Kavanagh states
That there's health and worth in any talk about
The properties of land. Sandy, glarry,
Mossy, heavy, cold, the actual soil
Almost doesn't matter; the main thing is
An inner restitution, a purchase come by
By pacing it in words that make you feel
You've found your feet in what "surefooted" means
And in the ground of your own understanding—
Like Heracles stepping in and standing under
Atlas's sky-lintel, as earthed and heady
As I am when I talk about the loose box.

·

And they found the infant wrapped in swaddling clothes
And laid in a manger.

                     But the plaster child in nappies,
Bare baby-breasted little *rigor vitae*,
Crook-armed, seed-nailed, nothing but gloss and chill—
He wasn't right at all.

                       And no hayrack
To be seen.

                    The solid stooping shepherds,
The stiff-lugged donkey, Joseph, Mary, each
Figure in the winter crib was well
And truly placed. There was even real straw
On the side-altar. And an out-of-scale,
Too crockery, kneeling cow. And fairy lights.
But no, no fodder-billowed armfuls spilling over . . .

At the altar rail I knelt and learnt almost
Not to admit the let-down to myself.

                        •

Stable child, grown stabler when I read
In adolescence Thomas *dolens* Hardy—

Not, oddly enough, his Christmas Eve night-piece
About the oxen in their bedded stall,
But the threshing scene in *Tess of the D'Urbervilles*—
That magnified my soul. Raving machinery,
The thresher bucking sky, rut-shuddery,
A headless Trojan horse expelling straw
From where the head should be, the underjaws
Like staircases set champing—it hummed and slugged
While the big sag and slew of the canvas belt
That would cut your head off if you didn't watch
Flowed from the flywheel. And comes flowing back,
The whole mote-sweaty havoc and mania
Of threshing day, the feeders up on top
Like pyre-high Aztec priests gutting forked sheaves
And paying them ungirded to the drum.

Slack of gulped straw, the belly-taut of seedbags.
And in the stilly night, chaff piled in ridges,
Earth raw where the four wheels rocked and battled.

•

Michael Collins, ambushed at Beal na Blath,
At the Pass of Flowers, the Blossom Gap, his own
Bloom-drifted, soft Avernus-mouth,
Has nothing to hold on to and falls again
Willingly, lastly, foreknowledgeably deep
Into the hay-floor that gave once in his childhood
Down through the bedded mouth of the loft trapdoor,
The loosening fodder-chute, the aftermath . . .

This has been told of Collins and retold
By his biographer:
                    One of his boy-deeds
Was to enter the hidden jaws of that hay crevasse
And get to his feet again and come unscathed
Through a dazzle of pollen scarves to breathe the air.
True or not true, the fall within his fall,
That drop through the flower-floor lets him find his feet
In an underworld of understanding
Better than any newsreel lying-in-state
Or footage of the laden gun-carriage
And grim cortege could ever manage to.

                    Or so it can be stated
In the must and drift of talk about the loose box.

Turpin Song

The horse pistol, we called it:
Brass inlay smooth in the stock,
Two hammers cocked like lugs,
Two mottled metal barrels,
Sooty nostrilled, levelled.

Bracketed over the door
Of the lower bedroom, a ghost
Heft that we longed to feel,
Two fingers on two triggers,
The full of your hand of haft.

Where was the Great North Road?
Who rode in a tricorn hat?
Bob Cushley with his jennet?
Ned Kane in his pony and trap?
The thing was out of place.

When I lift up my eyes at the start
Of Stanley Kubrick's film
A horse pistol comes tumbling
From over the door of the world
And it's nineteen forty-eight

Or -nine, we have transgressed,
We've got our hands on it
And it lies there, broken in bits.
Wind blows through the open hayshed.
I lift up my eyes with the apes.

The Border Campaign

for Nadine Gordimer

Soot-streaks down the courthouse wall, a hole
Smashed in the roof, the rafters in the rain
Still smouldering:
                 when I heard the word "attack"
In St. Columb's College in nineteen fifty-six
It left me winded, left nothing between me
And the sky that moved beyond my boarder's dormer
The way it would have moved the morning after
Savagery in Heorot, its reflection placid
In those waterlogged huge pawmarks Grendel left
On the boreen to the marsh.
                      All that was written
And to come I was a part of then,
At one with clan chiefs galloping down paths
To gaze at the talon Beowulf had nailed
High on the gable, the sky still moving grandly.

Every nail and claw-spike, every spur
And hackle and hand-barb on that heathen brute
Was like a steel prong in the morning dew.

"Nema problema!" The Macedonian
Taxi-driver screeched and the taxi screeched
At every unfenced corner on the pass,
Then accelerated.
         "Beria! Beria! Beria!"
Screeched Vladimir Chupeski, every time
He smashed a vodka glass and filled another
During those days and nights of '78
When we hardly ever sobered at the Struga
Poetry Festival.

        Rafael Alberti
Was "honouree" and Caj Westerburg,
A Finnish Hamlet in black corduroy,
Sweated "on principle" (or was that just projection
Of my northern tweed-wearer's contrariness?).

Also there: "Hans Magnus Enzensberger.
Unexpected. Sharp in panama hat,
Pressed-to-a-T cream linen suit. He gets
Away with it."
        And a soothsaying Dane
Of the avant-garde, squinting up at a squinch,
His eye as clear as the water and coral floor

Of Lake Ohrid. His first words to me were:
"Is this not you, these mosaics and madonnas?
You are a south. Your bogs were summer bogs."

●

In Belgrade I had found my west-in-east.

"Belmullet melancholy of huckster shops
And small shop windows. Unfresh bread, tinned peas.
Also Belmullet elders in the streets.
Black shawls, straight walk, the weather eye, the beads."

Then I saw men in fezes, left the known world
On the short and sweetening mud-slide of a coffee.

●

At the still centre of the cardinal points
The flypaper hung from our kitchen ceiling,
Honey-strip and death-trap, a barley-sugar twist
Of glut and loathing . . .
                              In a nineteen fifties
Of iron stoves and kin groups still in place,

Congregations blackening the length
And breadth of summer roads.

                               And now the refugees
Come loaded on tractor mudguards and farm carts,
On trailers, ruck-shifters, box-barrows, prams,
On sticks, on crutches, on each other's shoulders,
I see its coil again like a syrup of Styx,
An old gold world-chain the world keeps falling from
Into the cloud-boil of a camera lens.

Were we not made for summer, shade and coolness
And gazing through an open door at sunlight?
For paradise lost? Is that what I was taught?

                          •

That old sense of a tragedy going on
Uncomprehended, at the very edge
Of the usual, it never left me once . . .
A pity I didn't know then (for Caj's sake)
Hygo Simberg's allegory of Finland,
The one where the wounded angel's being carried
By two farm youngsters across an open field:
Marshland, estuary light, a farther shore

With factory chimneys. Is it the socialist thirties
Or the shale and slag and sloblands of great hurt?
A first communion angel with big white wings,
White bandage round her brow, white flowers in hand,
Holds herself in place on a makeshift stretcher
Between manchild number one in round soft hat
And manchild number two in a bumfreezer
And what could be his father's wellingtons.
Allegory, I say, but who's to know
How to read sorrow rightly, or at all?

                       ●

The open door, the jambs, the worn saddle
And actual granite of the doorstep slab.
Now enter another angel, fit as ever,
Past each house with a doorstep daubed "Serb house."

                       ●

How does the real get into the made-up?
Ask me an easier one.
                    But this much I do know:
Our taximan, for all his speed, was late

For the poetry reading we were meant to give
At a cement factory in the mountains.
So a liquid lunch with comrade managers
Ended in siesta and woozy wake-ups
Just before sunset. Then, the notebook says,
"People on the move, field full of folk,
Packhorses with panniers, uphill push
Of families, unending pilgrim stream.
To-day is workers' day in memory
Of General Strike. Also Greek Orthodox
Madonna's Day."
                    We followed a dry watercourse,
Rattling stones, subdued by the murmuring crowd
As darkness fell. We passed a water-blesser
On his rock apart, El Greco-gaunt and cinctured
("Magician," said Vladimir), waving his cross
Above the tins and jampotfuls held up.

Then on the mountaintop, outside a church,
Icons being carried, candles lit, flowers
And sweet basil in abundance, some kind of mass
Being celebrated behind the iconostasis,
A censer swung and carried through the crowd.
I had been there, I knew this, but was still

Haunted by it as by an unread dream.
The sale of holy objects. The little groups
Who'd walked all day now gathering in rings,
Allowing themselves a taste of their bread and olives.

·

As the Boeing's innards trembled and we climbed
Into the pure serene and protocols
Of Air Traffic Control, courtesy of Lufthansa,
I kept my seat belt fastened as instructed,
Smoked the minute the *No Smoking* went off
And took it as my due when wine was poured
By a slight *de haut en bas* of my headphoned head.
Nema problema. Ja. All systems go.

May 1999

1

And then at midnight as we started to descend
Into the burning valley of Gijon,
Into its blacks and crimsons, *in medias res*,
It was as if my own face burned again
In front of the fanned-up lip and crimson maw
Of a pile of newspapers lit long ago
One windy evening, breaking off and away
In flame-posies, small airborne fire-ships
Endangering the house-thatch and the stacks—
For we almost panicked there in the epic blaze
Of those furnaces and hot refineries
Where the night-shift worked on in their element
And we lost all hope of reading the map right
And gathered speed and cursed the hellish roads.

2

Next morning on the way to Piedras Blancas
I felt like a soul being prayed for.
I saw men cutting aftergrass with scythes,

Beehives in clover, a windlass and a shrine,
The maize like golden cargo in its hampers.
I was a pilgrim new upon the scene
Yet entering it as if it were home ground,
The Gaeltacht, say, in the nineteen fifties,
Where I was welcome, but of small concern
To families at work in the roadside fields
Who'd watch and wave at me from their other world
As was the custom still near Piedras Blancas.

3

At San Juan de las Harenas
It was a bright day of the body.
Two rivers flowed together under sunlight.
Watercourses scored the level sand.
The sea hushed and glittered outside the bar.
And in the afternoon, gulls *in excelsis*
Bobbed and flashed on air like altar boys
With their quick turns and tapers and responses
In the great re-echoing cathedral gloom
Of distant Compostela, *stela, stela.*

Ballynahinch Lake

Godi, fanciullo mio; stato soave,
Stagion lieta è cotesta.

—LEOPARDI, "Il Sabato del Villaggio"

for Eamon Grennan

So we stopped and parked in the spring-cleaning light
Of Connemara on a Sunday morning
As a captivating brightness held and opened
And the utter mountain mirrored in the lake
Entered us like a wedge knocked sweetly home
Into core timber.
                           Not too far away
But far enough for their rumpus not to carry,
A pair of waterbirds splashed up and down
And on and on. Next thing their strong white flex
That could have been excitement or the death-throes
Turned into lift-off, big sure sweeps and dips
Above the water—no rafter-skimming souls
Translating in and out of the house of life
But air-heavers, far heavier than the air.

Yet something in us had unhoused itself
At the sight of them, so that when she bent
To turn the key she only half-turned it
And spoke, as it were, directly to the windscreen,

In profile and in thought, the wheel at arm's length,
Averring that this time, yes, it had indeed
Been useful to stop; then inclined her driver's brow
Which shook a little as the ignition fired.

The Clothes Shrine

It was a whole new sweetness
In the early days to find
Light white muslin blouses
On a see-through nylon line
Drip-drying in the bathroom
Or a nylon slip in the shine
Of its own electricity—
As if St. Brigid once more
Had rigged up a ray of sun
Like the one she'd strung on air
To dry her own cloak on
(Hard-pressed Brigid, so
Unstoppably on the go)—
The damp and slump and unfair
Drag of the workaday
Made light of and got through
As usual, brilliantly.

Red, White and Blue

1. RED

What I loved about that much-snapped scarlet coat
Was the hunting jacket look of fitted waist
And tailored shoulder, the nifty, tricksy bounce
Of hemline hitting off your knee behind
And your knee in front.
                              "She's like a wee pony!"
Butter wouldn't melt in that smiler's mouth
So I smiled straight back, as who should say, "Good God,
You know you're absolutely right.
I love the go and gladsomeness in her,
Something unbroken, her gift for pure dismay
At shits like you."
                              And had the good fortune
To smile again into his peeky face
Later that night, as you jived with me hell for leather
In the Students Union, the cleared floor like a paddock
Where we gave each other rope and scope and snaffle.

"Redingote!" you'd cry.
                              And me, back, "Giddy up!"

2. WHITE

The screaming from the pool was bad enough,
Busloads of schoolkids coming in on rota
To the baths next door, the banshee acoustic
Of the glass-and-iron dome upping the wildness.
But in your state you thought the screaming came
From the labour ward.
                        At last-kiss, time-to-go time,
You were dry on the lips, hot-cheeked, already gone
Drifting away on the high berg of the bed.
They had given you a cut-off top of sorts,
Plain as a flour-bag, orphanage issue stuff,
White calico demure at the neckline
But unmistakably made for access
Elsewhere.
            Through its laundered weave
I tried to call you back but your quarantine
Was making you touch-proof and my hand
That thought it knew its way got lost and shied.
O where was the thick of thickets, the hug and birl
Of pleasures wrought to anger and beyond?
Ahead of us, my love, the small hours tournaments,
But that afternoon I left the lists and rode

From the sun-daunting keep of Castle Childbirth
And even though you knew as you lay contracting
Behind its bastions that the lilied moat
Was uncrossable, the drawbridge drawn up,
The battlements secure and audience
With the chatelaine denied, behind your eyes
Eye-tooth-tightened shut against the pangs,
What you still could not help making yourself see
Was the Knight of the White Feather turning tail.

3. BLUE

"Yes, pretty, *veh* pretty." How many times
Have you mimicked the entirely unaffected
And *veh* genuine touch of class she showed
In her praise of the gate-lodge and the avenue
At Castlebellingham. She was deigning
To bestow that much attention, and in the whim
Of her bestowals we felt ourselves included—
Hitchhikers who must have taken her fancy
Or her husband's, whom I then took to be
Officer class in civvies on weekend leave
In southern Ireland, as he called it.

                                        "Tell me,
I mean, you know, in southern Ireland,
Houses like that, are there many of them left?
Your crowd burnt the lot down, did they not,
In the nineteen twenties?"
                                        It then being
1963, we simply dived for cover,
("We're from the north,") or might surprise attack
With a quick torrent of the names of towns
Burnt in reprisal. But her "pretty, *veh* pretty,"
Said with the half-interest she might display
Later that night, letting her warm silks fall
In the lamplight of some coaching inn in Wicklow,
Was like a reminder a goddess might vouchsafe
To recall a hero to his ardent purpose.

Doves or no doves, it was a Venus car
We had thumbed down after more than half an hour
On the bridge outside Dundalk. You rose before them
In a Fair Isle tank-top and blue denim skirt
And denim jacket. And much blue eye make-up.

A Botticelli dressed down for the sixties.
So their big waxed Rolls flows softly to a halt,
The running board comes level with the footpath
And we are borne—sweet diction—south and south.

Virgil: Eclogue IX

LYCIDAS: Where are you headed, Moeris? Into town?

MOERIS: The things we have lived to see . . . The last thing
You could've imagined happening has happened.
An outsider lands and says he has the rights
To our bit of ground. "Out, old hands," he says,
"This place is mine." And these kid-goats in the creel—
Bad cess to him—these kids are his. All's changed.

LYCIDAS: The story I heard was about Menalcas,
How your song-man's singing saved the place,
Starting from where the hills go doubling back
And the ridge keeps sloping gently to the water,
Right down to those old scraggy-headed beech trees.

MOERIS: That's what you would have heard. But songs and tunes
Can no more hold out against brute force than doves
When eagles swoop. The truth is, Lycidas,
If I hadn't heard the crow caw on my left
In our hollow oak, I'd have kept on arguing
And that would've been the end of the road, for me
That's talking to you, and for Menalcas even.

LYCIDAS: Shocking times. Our very music, our one consolation,
Confiscated, all but. And Menalcas himself
Nearly one of the missing. Who would there be to sing
Praise songs to the nymphs? Who hymn the earth
To grow wild flowers and grass, and shade the wells
With overhanging green? Who sing the song
I listened to in silence the other day
And learned by heart as you went warbling it,
Off to the Amaryllis we all love?
The one that goes, "O herd my goats for me,
Tityrus, till I come back. I won't be long.
Graze them and then water them, and watch
The boyo with the horns doesn't go for you."

MOERIS: And then there was that one he never finished,
Addressed to Varus, about a choir of swans
Chanting his name to the stars, "should Mantua
Survive, Mantua too close to sad Cremona."

LYCIDAS: If you've any song to sing, then sing it now
So that your bees may swerve off past the yew trees,
Your cows in clover thrive with canted teats
And tightening udders. The Pierian muses
Made me a poet too, I too have songs,

And people in the country call me bard,
But I'm not sure: I have done nothing yet
That Varius or Cinna would take note of.
I'm a squawking goose among sweet-throated swans.

MOERIS: I'm quiet because I'm trying to piece together
As best I can a song I think you'd know:
"Galatea," it goes, "come here to me.
What's in the sea and the waves that keeps you spellbound?
Here earth breaks out in wildflowers, she rills and rolls
The streams in waterweed, here poplars bend
Where the bank is undermined and vines in thickets
Are meshing shade with light. Come here to me.
Let the mad white horses paw and pound the shore."

LYCIDAS: There was something I heard you singing by yourself
One night when the sky was clear. I have the air
So maybe I'll get the words. "Daphnis, Daphnis, why
Do you concentrate your gaze on the old stars?
Look for the star of Caesar, rising now,
Star of corn in the fields and hay in haggards,
Of clustered grapes gone purple in the heat
On hillsides facing south. Daphnis, now is the time
To plant the pear slips for your children's children."

MOERIS: Age robs us of everything, of our very mind.
Many a time I remember as a boy
Serenading the slow sun down to rest,
But nowadays I'm forgetting song after song
And my voice is going: maybe the wolves have blinked it.
But Menalcas will keep singing and keep the songs.

LYCIDAS: Come on, don't make excuses, I want to hear you
And now's your chance, now this hush has fallen
Everywhere—look—on the plain, and every breeze
Has calmed and quietened. We've come half-way.
Already you can see Bianor's tomb
Just up ahead. Here where they've trimmed and faced
The old green hedge, here's where we're going to sing.
Set that creel and those kid-goats on the ground.
We'll make it into town in all good time.
Or if it looks like rain when it's getting dark,
Singing shortens the road, so we'll walk and sing.
Walk then, Moeris, and sing. I'll take the kids.

MOERIS: That's enough of that, my boy. We've a job to do.
When the real singer comes, we'll sing in earnest.

Glanmore Eclogue

MYLES: A house and ground. And your own bay tree as well
And time to yourself. You've landed on your feet.
If you can't write now, when will you ever write?

POET: A woman changed my life. Call her Augusta
Because we arrived in August, and from now on
This month's baled hay and blackberries and combines
Will spell Augusta's bounty.

MYLES: Outsiders own
The country nowadays, but even so
I don't begrudge you. You're Augusta's tenant
And that's enough. She has every right,
Maybe more right than most, to her quarter acre.
She knows the big glen inside out, and everything
Meliboeus ever wrote about it,
All the tramps he met tramping the roads
And all he picked up, listening in a loft
To servant girls colloguing in the kitchen.
Talk about changed lives! Those were the days—
Land Commissions making tenants owners,
Empire taking note at last too late . . .
But now with all this money coming in
And peace being talked up, the boot's on the other foot.

First it was Meliboeus' people
Went to the wall, now it will be us.
Small farmers here are priced out of the market.

POET: Backs to the wall and empty pockets: Meliboeus
Was never happier than when he was on the road
With people on their uppers. Loneliness
Was his passport through the world. Midge-angels
On the face of water, the first drop before thunder,
A stranger on a wild night, *out in the rain falling.*
His spirit lives for me in things like that.

MYLES: Book-learning is the thing. You're a lucky man.
No stock to feed, no milking times, no tillage
Nor blisters on your hand nor weather-worries.

POET: Meliboeus would have called me "Mr Honey."

MYLES: Our old language that Meliboeus learnt
Has lovely songs. What about putting words
On one of them, words that the rest of us
Can understand, and singing it here and now?

POET: I have this summer song for the glen and you:

Early summer, cuckoo cuckoos,
Welcome, summer is what he sings.
Heather breathes on soft bog-pillows.
Bog-cotton bows to moorland wind.

The deer's heart skips a beat; he startles.
The sea's tide fills, it rests, it runs.
Season of the drowsy ocean.
Tufts of yellow-blossoming whins.

Bogbanks shine like ravens' wings.
The cuckoo keeps on calling *Welcome*.
The speckled fish jumps; and the strong
Warrior is up and running.

A little nippy chirpy fellow
Hits the highest note there is;
The lark sings out his clear tidings.
Summer, shimmer, perfect days.

Sonnets from Hellas

1. INTO ARCADIA

It was opulence and amen on the mountain road.
Walnuts bought on a high pass from a farmer
Who'd worked in Melbourne once and now trained water
Through a system of pipes and runnels of split reed
Known in Hellas, probably, since Hesiod—
That was the least of it. When we crossed the border
From Argos into Arcadia, and farther
Into Arcadia, a lorry load
Of apples had burst open on the road
So that for yards our tyres raunched and scrunched them
But we drove on, juiced up and fleshed and spattered,
Revelling in it. And then it was the goatherd
With his goats in the forecourt of the filling station,
Subsisting beyond eclogue and translation.

2. CONKERS

All along the dank, sunk, rock-floored lane
To the acropolis in Sparta, we couldn't help
Tramping on burst shells and crunching down
The high-gloss horse-chestnuts. I thought of kelp
And foals' hooves, bladderwort, dubbed leather
As I bent to gather them, a hint of ordure
Coming and going off their tainted pith.
Cyclopic stone on each side of the path.
Rings of defence. Breached walls. The looted conkers
Gravid in my satchel, swinging nicely.
Then a daylight moon appeared behind Dimitri
As he sketched and squared his shoulders like a centaur's
And nodded, nodded, nodded towards the spouses,
Heard but not seen behind much thick acanthus.

Barbounia schooled below the balcony—
Shadows on shelving sand in sandy Pylos.
Wave-clip and flirt, tide-slap and flop and flow:
I woke to the world there like Telemachos,
Young again in the whitewashed light of morning
That flashed on the ceiling like an early warning
From myself to be more myself in the mast-bending
Marine breeze, to key the understanding
To that image of the bow strung as a lyre
Robert Fitzgerald spoke of: Harvard Nestor,
Sponsor and host, translator of all Homer,
His wasted face in profile, ceiling-staring
As he schooled me in the course, not yet past caring,
Scanning the offing. Far-seeing shadower.

4. THE AUGEAN STABLES

My favourite bas-relief: Athene showing
Heracles where to broach the river bank
With a nod of her high helmet, her staff sunk
In the exact spot, the Alpheus flowing
Out of its course into the deep dung strata
Of King Augeas' reeking yard and stables.
Sweet dissolutions from the water tables,
Blocked doors and packed floors deluging like gutters . . .
And it was there in Olympia, down among green willows,
The lustral wash and run of river shallows,
That we heard of Sean Brown's murder in the grounds
Of Bellaghy GAA Club. And imagined
Hose-water smashing hard back off the asphalt
In the car park where his athlete's blood ran cold.

5. CASTALIAN SPRING

Thunderface. Not Zeus's ire, but hers
Refusing entry, and mine mounting from it.
This one thing I had vowed: to drink the waters
Of the Castalian Spring, to arrogate
That much to myself and be the poet
Under the god Apollo's giddy cliff—
But the inner water sanctum was roped off
When we arrived. Well then, to hell with that,
And to hell with all who'd stop me, thunderface!
So up the steps then, into the sandstone grottoes,
The seeps and dreeps, the shallow pools, the mosses,
Come from beyond, and come far, with this useless
Anger draining away, on terraces
Where I bowed and mouthed in sweetness and defiance.

6. DESFINA

Mount Parnassus placid on the skyline:
Slieve na mBard, Knock Filiocht, Ben Duan.
We gaelicized new names for Poetry Hill
As we wolfed down horta, tarama and houmos
At sunset in the farmyard, drinking ouzos,
Pretending not to hear the Delphic squeal
Of the streel-haired *cailleach* in the scullery.
Then it was time to head into Desfina
To allow them to sedate her. And so retsina,
Anchovies, squid, dolmades, french fries even.
My head was light, I was hyper, boozed, borean
As we bowled back down towards the olive plain
Siren-tyred and manic on the horn
Round hairpin bends looped like boustrophedon.

The Gaeltacht

I wish, *mon vieux*, that you and Barlo and I
Were back in Rosguill, on the Atlantic Drive,
And that it was again nineteen sixty
And Barlo was alive

And Paddy Joe and Chips Rafferty and Dicky
Were there talking Irish, for I believe
In that case Aoibheann Marren and Margaret Conway
And M. and M. and Deirdre Morton and Niamh

Would be there as well. And it would be great too
If we could see ourselves, if the people we are now
Could hear what we were saying, and if this sonnet

In imitation of Dante's, where he's set free
In a boat with Lapo and Guido, with their girlfriends in it,
Could be the wildtrack of our gabble above the sea.

The Real Names

for Brian Friel

Enter Owen Kelly, loping and gowling,
His underlip and lower jaw ill-set,
A mad turn in his eye, his shot-putter's
Neck and shoulders still a schoolboy's.
                              The hard sticks
He dumped down at the opening of the scene
Raised a stour off the boards, his turnip fists
Swung low out of his ripped tarpaulin smock.
I won't forget his Sperrins Caliban,
His bag-aproned, potato-gatherer's Shakespeare:
And I with my long nails will dig thee pig-nuts.

•

Who played Miranda?
                    Some junior-final dayboy.
Flaxen, credible, incredible
In a braided wig and costume, speaking high,
He was a she angelic in the light
We couldn't take our eyes off.
                              House lights down,
Liam McLelland enters, Ferdinand
Sleepwalking to the music, spied upon
By Gerry O'Neill cloaked up as Prospero.

"A voice like an organ, so he has, that boy,"
Gallagher (who directed) soliloquized
To the class next day.
                              The previous year
Gerry had been Macbeth, green football socks
Cross-gartered to his Thane of Cawdor knees.
And Anthony Murray, with the hiccups, played
The porter in an ignorant Scotch accent.

●

The smell of the new book. The peep ahead
At words not quite beyond you. At which time
A CARRIER, with a lantern in his hand
Entered the small hours, speaking low-life prose,
And a light that sparked when I read that Charles's Wain
Was *over the new chimney* has never stopped
Arriving ever since.
                              Pinhead words
In the thick sable of the universe.
Single line to sing along the lifeline.
Sometimes it was as if a chink had opened
Upon a scene foreseen and enterable—
Like the perpetual that shone in the sparks going up

From MacNicholl's chimney:

> I was crossing the yard
When I saw them that one time,
Babe in the world, up to my eyes in it,
Up and about in the winter milker's darkness,
Hand held by one with a lantern in her hand.

●

Shakespeare's father (or so John Aubrey claims)
Was a butcher, and when Shakespeare was a boy
"He exercised his father's trade, but when
He kill'd a Calfe, he would doe it in *high style*
& make a speech."

> Airiness from the start,
Me on top of the byre, seeing things
In a headier light from that much nearer heaven,
Managing to stand up unsupported
On the deck-tilt of hot zinc: I'm on a roof
That overlooks forever, with a pretend
Gully knife of my own in one raised hand,
Sawing air with the other

> (Call it a stage
That everyone goes through ahead of time).

Cows snuffle at feed buckets in the byre,
The stall-chains clink.

                    Call it a home from home.

                         •

There is a willow grows askaunt the brook
But in the beginning it was "sally tree."
Sallies in hedges and sallies on the bank
Of the Moyola River and black sallies
Like a line of daunted stragglers bogging down
In the sedge and glarry wetness of our meadow.
The one in the yard was tetter-barked and hollow,
Two-timing earth and air: corona top
Of flick-and-shimmer, sprout-and-tremble growth.
Land and sky assembled themselves round it.
In the protocol of soul, soul might have moved
Backwards away from it, as from a monarch,
Then turned to those princess-saplings by the river.
But they in their turn had stepped a word away
And willowed like Ophelias in Moyola.

•

"Frankie McMahon, you're Bassanio.
Irwin, Launcelot Gobbo. Bredin, Portia."
That was the cast, or some of it; the scene,
The righthand side of Gallagher's low desk,
A nowhere where the three caskets were placed
In dumb-show. And off we went again. (And yes,
Of course, Irwin the fabulous
Who'd walked out of the gates on the first day
Was typecast as the runaway apprentice.
And Cassoni the Italian as Lorenzo).
But who was Jessica?
                        Unforgotten,
Out of this world, the start of Act Five, Scene One.
"*In such a night*—continue, please, Cassoni!"
"—*Stood Dido with a willow in her hand
Upon the wild sea banks.*"
                        In summer's language.
In 1954. In the sun-thwarted
Glass and steel of those new showpiece classrooms.

*

Duncan's horses, plastered in wet, surge up
Wild as the chestnut tree one terrible night
In Mossbawn, the aerial rod like a mast
Whiplashed in tempest, my mother rocking and oching
And blessing herself—

                the breach in nature open
As the back of the raiders' lorry hammering on
For the Monaghan border, blood loosed in a scrim
From the tailboard, the volunteer screaming *O Jesus!*
O merciful Jesus.

            Or was it the night
The *Princess Victoria* was lost, when the words *sink*
And *gale-force* and *drowning* broke from their stalls
And whinnied round window and chimney?

                      The newsreader's
Voice abreast of the nightmare, striding the airwaves.

*

Romantic England live and well. *Twelfth Night*
In open evening air in Regent's Park.
Feste's sad counter-tenor and hugged lute

Erotic as it got. In such a dark
McCoo, McAuley, Terrins, me, half tight
In the small hours fug of an Earls Court student flat . . .
In love with love. And scrumpy. And the bright
Glamour of that phosphorescent mark
They stamped on your hand in *Café des Artistes*.

●

Feste, for all the world like an "ESN"
From Class 1G, those little gutsy suede-heads
I took for PT, Fridays, 2 to 3,
By the cemetery short-cut to Falls Park
And let go early. And then went myself . . .

Feste, with his ear to his instrument
And eye on nothing, like the deaf boy in 5A
With his bud-pale hearing aid and clean school tie
And panic when I swooped. "Sir, no! Please, sir!"

Feste, like catatonic Bobby X
With his curled-in shoulders and cabbage-water eyes
Speechlessly rocking, *a little tiny boy*
Shut up inside him. And the doctor shouting,

"Bobby, for Christ's sake, Bobby, catch yourself on."
Me in attendance, watching sorrow's elf
Bow his head and hunch and stay beyond us,
Like that moment at the end when *"Exeunt*
[All but FESTE*]*. FESTE *(sings)*."
                              But not Bobby sings.

                              *

Then say *chameleon*. And the boy-men reappear
Who's whoing themselves like changelings.
                              So will it be

Ariel or the real name, the already
Featly sweetly tuneful Philip Coulter?
Or his brother Joe as Banquo, dressed in white,
Wise Joe, good Banquo, fairest of the prefects?
Aura and justice, soul in bliss or torment,
Ghost on cue at the banquet, entering
And entering memory like mitigation—
The table on stage a long, formica-topped
Table for fourteen, on loan from the refectory
Where we, in fourteens, moon-calves, know-nothings
Stood by our chairs and waited for the grace.

The Bookcase

Ashwood or oakwood? Planed to silkiness,
Mitred, much eyed-along, each vellum-pale
Board in the bookcase held and never sagged.
Virtue went forth from its very ship-shapeness.

Whoever remembers the rough blue paper bags
Loose sugar was once sold in might remember
The jacket of (was it Oliver & Boyd's?)
Collected Hugh MacDiarmid. And the skimmed milk

Bluey-white of the Chatto Selected
Elizabeth Bishop. Murex of Macmillan's
Collected Yeats. And their Collected Hardy.
Yeats of "Memory." Hardy of "The Voice."

Voices too of Frost and Wallace Stevens
Off a Caedmon double album, off different shelves.
Dylan at full volume, the Bushmills killed.
"Do Not Go Gentle." "Don't be going yet."

•

Heavy as the gate I hung on once
As it swung its arc through air round to the hedge-back,

The bookcase turns on a druggy hinge, its load
Divulging into a future perfect tense

Where we hang loose, ruminating and repeating
The three words, "books from Ireland," to each other,
Quoting for pleasure the Venerable Bede
Who writes in his *History of the English Church*

That scrapings off the leaves of books from Ireland
When steeped in water palliate the effect
Of snake-bite. "For on this isle," he states,
"Almost everything confers immunity."

●

Chiefly I liked the lines and weight of it.
A measuredness. Its long back to the wall
And carpentered right angles I could feel
In my neck and shoulder. And books from everywhere.

Cash in *As I Lay Dying* makes a coffin—
For thirteen stated reasons—"on the bevel."
From first, "There is more surface for the nails
To grip," to last, "It makes a better job."

In *Riders to the Sea* Synge specifies
In the opening stage direction "some new boards
Standing by the wall," and in Maurya's speech
"White boards" are like storm-gleams on the flood

At the very end, or the salt salvaged makings
Of a raft for books, a bier to be borne.
I imagine us bracing ourselves for the first lift,
Then staggering for balance, it has grown so light.

Vitruviana

for Felim Egan

In the deep pool at Portstewart, I waded in
Up to the chest, then stood there half-suspended
Like Vitruvian man, both legs wide apart,
Both arms out buoyant to the fingertips,
Oxter-cogged on water.
                    My head was light,
My backbone plumb, my boy-nipples bisected
And tickled by the steel-zip cold meniscus.

●

On the hard scrabble of the Junior football pitch
Where Leo Day, the college "drillie," bounced
And counted and kept us all in line
In front of the wooden horse—"*One! Two! In! Out!*"—
We upped and downed and scissored arms and legs
And spread ourselves on the wind's cross, felt our palms
As tautly strung as Francis of Assisi's
In Giotto's mural, where angelic neon
Zaps the ping-palmed saint with the stigmata.

On Sandymount Strand I can connect
Some bits and pieces. My seaside whirligig.
The cardinal points. The grey matter of sand
And sky. And a light that is down to earth
Beginning to fan out and open up.

Ten Glosses

1. THE MARCHING SEASON

"What bloody man is that?" "A drum, a drum!"
Prepossessed by what I know by heart,
I wait for Banquo and Macbeth to come
Unbowed, on cue, and scripted from the start.

2. THE CATECHISM

Q. and A. come back. They "formed my mind."
"Who is my neighbour?" "My neighbour is all mankind."

3. THE BRIDGE

Steady under strain and strong through tension,
Its feet on both sides but in neither camp,
It stands its ground, a span of pure attention,
A holding action, the arches and the ramp
Steady under strain and strong through tension.

4. A SUIT

"I'll make you one," he said, "and balance it
Perfectly on you." So I could almost feel
The plumb line of the creased tweed hit my heel,

My shoulders like a spar or arms of a scale
Under the jacket, my whole shape realigned
In ways that suited me down to the ground.

So although a suit was the last thing that I needed
I weighed his words and wore them and decided
There and then it was going for a song.

5. THE PARTY

Overheard at the party, like wet snow
That slumps down off a roof, the unexpected,
Softly powerful name of Wilfred Owen.
Mud in your eye. Artillery in heaven.

6. W. H. AUDEN, 1907–73

After Oxford and Iceland and Spain and Berlin and Freud,
After Marx and the Thirties, it was New York and Chester and
    God.
A pause for po-ethics. The moral ascent of Parnassus.
Then retrenchment, libretti, martinis, the slippers, the face.
Conceived in the Danelaw, a language shift and a ruction,
He was barker of stanzas, a star turn, a source of instruction,
And the definite growth rings of genius rang in his voice.

7. THE LESSON

According to Hammond, who heard it out on a spree
From a man who had known the priest who was chaplain on duty
The morning the last man was hanged in Crumlin Road Jail,
What the man said as he shook hands and went to the hangman
Was, "Father, this is going to be a lesson to me."

8. MOLING'S GLOSS

Among my elders, I know better
    And frown on any carry-on;
Among the brat-pack on the batter
    I'm taken for a younger man.

from the Irish

9. COLLY

Niamh's horse for Oisin was grand, but saddle me colly,
Giddy on wind and black as the hair on King Billy,

Chimney flakes flecking the air, carbon-dotting the white
Wash on the line, a fly-past, a freak-out of soot.

10. A NORMAN SIMILE

To be marvellously yourself like the river water
Gerald of Wales says runs in Arklow harbour
Even at high tide when you'd expect salt water.

The Fragment

"Light came from the east," he sang,
"Bright guarantee of God, and the waves went quiet.
I could see headlands and buffeted cliffs.
                    Often, for marked courage, fate spares the man
It has not marked already."

And when their objection was reported to him—
That he had gone to bits and was leaving them
Nothing to hold on to, his first and last lines
Neither here nor there—
                    "Since when," he asked,
"Are the first line and last line of any poem
Where the poem begins and ends?"

On His Work in the English Tongue

in memory of Ted Hughes

1

Post-this, post-that, post-the-other, yet in the end
Not past a thing. Not understanding or telling
Or forgiveness.
     But often past oneself,
Pounded like a shore by the roller griefs
In language that can still knock language sideways.

2

I read it quickly, then stood looking back
As if it were a bridge I had passed under—
The single span and bull's-eye of the one
Over the railway lines at Anahorish—
So intimate in there, the tremor-drip
And cranial acoustic of the stone
With its arch-ear to the ground, a listening post
Open to the light, to the limen world
Of soul on its lonely path, the rails on either side
Shining in silence, the fretful part of me
So steadied by their cogged and bolted stillness

I felt like one come out of an upper room
To fret no more and walk abroad confirmed.

3

Passive suffering: who said it was disallowed
As a theme for poetry? Already in *Beowulf*
The dumbfounding of woe, the stunt and stress
Of hurt-in-hiding is the best of it—
As when King Hrethel's son accidentally kills
His older brother and snaps the grief-trap shut
On Hrethel himself, wronged father of the son
Struck down, constrained by love and blood
To seek redress from the son who had survived—

And the poet draws from his word-hoard a weird tale
Of a life and a love balked, which I reword here
Remembering earth-tremors once on Dartmoor,
The power station wailing in its pit
Under the heath, as if our night walk led
Not to the promised tor but underground
To sullen halls where encumbered sleepers groaned.

4

"Imagine this pain: an old man
Lives to see his son's body
Swing on the gallows. He begins to keen
And weep for his boy, while the black raven
Gloats where he hangs: he can be of no help.
The wisdom of age is worthless to him.
Morning after morning he wakes to remember
That his child has gone; he has no interest
In living on until another heir
Is born in the hall, now that this boy
Has entered the door of death forever.
He gazes sorrowfully at his son's dwelling,
The banquet hall bereft of all delight,
The windswept hearthstone; the horsemen are sleeping,
The warriors under earth; what was is no more.
No tune from harp, no cheering in the yard.
Alone with his longing, he lies down on his bed
And sings a lament; everything is too large,
The steadings and the fields.
                              Such were the woes
And griefs endured by that doomed lord

After what happened. The king was helpless
To set to right the wrong committed . . ."

5

Soul has its scruples. Things not to be said.
Things for keeping, that can keep the small hours gaze
Open and steady. Things for the *aye* of God
And for poetry. Which is, as Milosz says,
"A dividend from ourselves," a tribute paid
By what we have been true to. A thing allowed.

Audenesque

in memory of Joseph Brodsky

Joseph, yes, you know the beat.
Wystan Auden's metric feet
Marched to it, unstressed and stressed,
Laying William Yeats to rest.

Therefore, Joseph, on this day,
Yeats's anniversary,
(Double-crossed and death-marched date,
January twenty-eight),

Its measured ways I tread again
Quatrain by constrained quatrain,
Meting grief and reason out
As you said a poem ought.

Trochee, trochee, falling: thus
Grief and metre order us.
Repetition is the rule,
Spins on lines we learnt at school.

Repetition, too, of cold
In the poet and the world,
Dublin Airport locked in frost,
Rigor mortis in your breast.

Ice no axe or book will break,
No Horatian ode unlock,
No poetic foot imprint,
Quatrain shift or couplet dint,

Ice of Archangelic strength,
Ice of this hard two-faced month,
Ice like Dante's in deep hell
Makes your heart a frozen well.

Pepper vodka you produced
Once in western Massachusetts
With the reading due to start
Warmed my spirits and my heart

But no vodka, cold or hot,
Aquavit or uisquebaugh
Brings the blood back to your cheeks
Or the colour to your jokes,

Politically incorrect
Jokes involving sex and sect,
Everything against the grain,
Drinking, smoking like a train.

In a train in Finland we
Talked last summer happily,
Swapping manuscripts and quips,
Both of us like cracking whips

Sharpened up and making free,
Heading west for Tampere
(West that meant for you, of course,
Lenin's train-trip in reverse).

Nevermore that wild speed-read,
Nevermore your tilted head
Like a deck where mind took off
With a mind-flash and a laugh,

Nevermore that rush to pun
Or to hurry through all yon
Jammed enjambements piling up
As you went above the top,

Nose in air, foot to the floor,
Revving English like a car
You hijacked when you robbed its bank
(Russian was your reserve tank).

Worshipped language can't undo
Damage time has done to you:
Even your peremptory trust
In words alone here bites the dust.

Dust-cakes, still—see *Gilgamesh*—
Feed the dead. So be their guest.
Do again what Auden said
Good poets do: bite, break their bread.

To the Shade of Zbigniew Herbert

You were one of those from the back of the north wind
Whom Apollo favoured and would keep going back to
In the winter season. And among your people you
Remained his herald whenever he'd departed
And the land was silent and summer's promise thwarted.
You learnt the lyre from him and kept it tuned.

"Would They Had Stay'd"

I

The colour of meadow hay, with its meadow-sweet
And liver-spotted dock leaves, they were there
Before we noticed them, all eyes and evening,
Up to their necks in the meadow.

                             "Where? I still can't—"
"There."
        "Oh yes. Of course, yes. Lovely."
                                     And they didn't
Move away.
        There, like the air agog.
The step of light on grass, halted mid-light.
Heartbeat and pupil. A match for us. And watching.

II

Norman MacCaig, come forth from the deer of Magdalen,
Those startlers standing still in fritillary land,
Heather-sentries far from the heath. Be fawn
To the redcoat, gallowglass in the Globe,
Tidings of trees that walked and were seen to walk.

(They did not move and he did not come forth.)

III

"Deer on the high hills":
Englished Iain MacGabhainn
Goes into linked verse—
Goes where the spirit listeth—
On its perfectly sure feet.

And Shakespeare's "Into
The air, as breath into the
Wind. Would they had stay'd!"
That too. And Iain's poem
Where sorrow just sits and rocks.

IV

Sorley MacLean. A mirage. A stag on a ridge
In the western desert above the burnt-out tanks.

V

What George Mackay Brown saw was a drinking deer
That glittered by the water. The human soul
In mosaic. Wet celandine and ivy.
Allegory hard as a figured shield
Smithied in Orkney for Christ's sake and Crusades,
Polished until its undersurface surfaced
Like peat smoke mulling through Byzantium.

Late in the Day

Sir William Wilde, in his *Beauties of the Boyne*,
Tells of a monk of Clonard, working late,
How when his candle burnt out, his quill pen
Feathered itself with a miraculous light

So he could go on working. Shadow-flit,
Ink-gleam and quill-shine, late now in the day
I need their likes, freshets and rivulets
Starting from nowhere, capillaries of joy

Frittered and flittering like the scimitar
Of cowpiss in the wind that David Thomson
Flashed on my inner eye from the murky byre
Where he imagined himself a cow let out in spring

Smelling green weed, up to his hips in grass.
Dark-roomed David, author of the memoir
Nairn in Darkness and Light, whose injured eyes
Saw waves and waterfalls in young girls' hair,

The glee of boyhood still alive and kicking
In the tattered stick-man I would meet and read
A lifetime later—erotic fancy-tickler,
Never more at home than when on the road,

Led by amazement as if it were a seal
Walking ahead of him up the Aran shingle
In a clawhammer coat and top hat, dressed to kill,
About to enter a public house or kitchen

The way he would himself, like Arion
Arriving in off the waves, off the dolphin's back,
Oblivious-seeming, but taking it all in
And glad of another chance to believe his luck.

Arion

We were all hard at it in the boat,
Some of us up tightening sail,
Some down at the heave and haul
Of the rowing benches, deeply cargoed,
Steady keeled, our passage silent,
The helmsman buoyant at the helm;
And I, who took it all for granted,
Sang to the sailors.
                Then turbulent
Sudden wind, a maelstrom:
The helmsman and the sailors perished.
Only I, still singing, washed
Ashore by the long sea-swell, sing on,
A mystery to my poet self,
And safe and sound beneath a rock shelf
Have spread my wet clothes in the sun.

from the Russian of Alexander Pushkin

Bodies and Souls

1. IN THE AFTERLIFE

It will be like following Jim Logue, the caretaker,
As he goes to sweep our hair off that classroom floor
Where the school barber set up once a fortnight,
Falling into step as he does his rounds,
Glimmerman of dorms and silent landings,
Of the refectory with its solid, crest-marked delph,
The ground-floor corridor, the laundry pile
And boots tagged for the cobbler. Was that your name
On a label? Were you a body or a soul?

2. NIGHTS OF '57

It wasn't asphodel but mown grass
We practised on each night after night prayers
When we lapped the college front lawn in bare feet,

Heel-bone and heart-thud, open-mouthed for summer.
The older I get, the quicker and the closer
I hear those labouring breaths and feel the coolth.

3. THE BEREAVED

Set apart. First out down the aisle
Like brides. Or those boys who were permitted
To leave the study early for music practice—
Privileged and unenvied, left alone
In the four bare walls to face the exercise,
Eyes shut, shoulders straight back, cold hands out
Above the keys. And then the savagery
Of the piano music's music going wrong.

Clonmany to Ahascragh

in memory of Rory Kavanagh

Now that the rest of us have no weeping left
These things will do it for you:
Willows standing out on Leitrim Moss,
Wounds that "wept" in the talk of those before you,
Rained-on statues from Clonmany to Ahascragh,
Condensation on the big windows
And walls of a school corridor in Derry
Where I drew with warm fingers once upon a time
To make a face that wept itself away
Down cold black glass.

Compose yourself again. And listen to me.
You were never up here in my attic study
Beyond the landing, up the second stairwell,
Step-ladder steep, and deep, and leading back
Down to the life going on.

                           Even so, appear
Till I tell you my good dream.

                                 Be at the door
I opened in the sleepwall when a green
Hurl of flood overwhelmed me and poured out
Lithe seaweed and a tumult of immense

Green cabbage roses into the downstairs.
No feeling of drowning panicked me, no let-up
In the attic downpour happened, no
Fullness could ever equal it, so flown
And sealed I feared it would be lost
If I put it into words.

                                But with you there at the door
I can tell it and can weep.

                      •

And if ever tears are to be wiped away,
It will be in river country,
In that confluence of unmarked bridge-rumped roads
Beyond the Shannon, between the River Suck
And the Corrib River, where a plentiful
Solitude floods everyone who drives
In the unseasonal warmth of a January afternoon
Into places battened down under oyster light,
Under names unknown to most, but available
To you and proclaimable by you
Like a man speaking in tongues, brought to his senses
By a sudden plout on the road into Ahascragh.

Sruth

in memory of Mary O Muirithe

The bilingual race
And truth of that water
Spilling down Errigal,

The *sruth* like the rush
Of its downpour translated
Into your accent:

You in your *dishabills*
Washing your face
In the guttural glen.

Mountain and maiden.
The shard of a mirror.
Your head in the air

Of that childhood *breac-Ghaeltacht*,
Those sky-maiden haunts
You would tell me about

Again and again—
Then asked me to visit:
If anything happened

Just to see and be sure
And not to forget
For your sake to do it.

Splash of clear water.
Things out in the open.
The spoken word, "cancer."

And now it has happened
I see what I saw
On the morning you asked me:

Neck-baring snowdrops—
Like you at the *sruth*—
First-footing springtime,

Fit for what comes.

Seeing the Sick

Anointed and all, my father did remind me
Of Hopkins's Felix Randal.

                              And then he grew
(As he would have said himself) "wee in his clothes"—
Spectral, a relict—

                        And seemed to have grown so
Because of something spectral he'd thrown off,
The unbelonging, moorland part of him
That was Northumbrian, the bounden he
Who had walked the streets of Hexham at eighteen
With his stick and task of bringing home the dead
Body of his uncle by cattle-ferry.

Ghost-drover from the start. Brandisher of keel.

None of your fettled and bright battering sandal.

Cowdung coloured tweed and ox-blood leather.

                              •

The assessor's eye, the tally-keeper's head
For what beasts were on what land in what year . . .
But then that went as well. And all precaution.

His smile a summer half-door opening out
And opening in. A reprieving light.
For which the tendered morphine had our thanks.

Electric Light

Candle-grease congealed, dark-streaked with wick-soot . . .
The smashed thumb-nail
Of that ancient mangled thumb was puckered pearl,

Rucked quartz, a littered Cumae.
In the first house where I saw electric light
She sat with her fur-lined felt slippers unzipped,

Year in, year out, in the same chair, and whispered
In a voice that at its loudest did nothing else
But whisper. We were both desperate

The night I was left to stay, when I wept and wept
Under the clothes, under the waste of light
Left turned on in the bedroom. "What ails you, child,

What ails you, for God's sake?" Urgent, sibilant
Ails, far off and old. Scaresome cavern waters
Lapping a boatslip. Her helplessness no help.

Lisp and relapse. Eddy of sybilline English.
Splashes between a ship and dock, to which,
Animula, I would come alive in time

As ferries churned and turned down Belfast Lough
Towards the brow-to-glass transport of a morning train,
The very "there-you-are-and-where-are-you?"

Of poetry itself. Backs of houses
Like the back of hers, meat-safes and mangles
In the railway-facing yards of fleeting England,

Then fields of grain like the Field of the Cloth of Gold.
To Southwark too I came, from tube-mouth into sunlight,
Moyola-breath by Thames's "straunge stronde."

If I stood on the bow-backed chair, I could reach
The light switch. They let me and they watched me.
A touch of the little pip would work the magic.

A turn of their wireless knob and light came on
In the dial. They let me and they watched me
As I roamed at will the stations of the world.

Then they were gone and Big Ben and the news
Were over. The set had been switched off,
All quiet behind the blackout except for

Knitting needles ticking, wind in the flue.
She sat with her fur-lined felt slippers unzipped,
Electric light shone over us, I feared

The dirt-tracked flint and fissure of her nail,
So plectrum-hard, glit-glittery, it must still keep
Among beads and vertebrae in the Derry ground.